I DARE YOU TO LIVE

*Reclaim Your Life From the
Grips of Strongholds*

Tuere Dunton-Forbes

Cover designed by J. Dortch Graphic Designs

Scripture taken from the New King James Version®. Copyright © 1982 by Thomas Nelson. Used by permission. All rights reserved.

All Scripture quotations are taken from *THE MESSAGE*, copyright © 1993, 2002, 2018 by Eugene H. Peterson. Used by permission of NavPress. All rights reserved. Represented by Tyndale House Publishers, Inc.

The Living Bible copyright © 1971 by Tyndale House Foundation. Used by permission of Tyndale House Publishers Inc., Carol Stream, Illinois 60188. All rights reserved. The Living Bible, TLB, and the The Living Bible logo are registered trademarks of Tyndale House Publishers.

Printed in the United States of America

First Printing: November 2021
The Scribe Tribe Publishing Group

THE SCRIBE TRIBE
PUBLISHING GROUP

ISBN (print) 978-1-7376411-6-2
ISBN (electronic) 978-1-7376411-7-9

To my **mother**, Kolette S. Nelloms, whose unconditional love was her greatest strength and her pain. To my **daddy**, John W. Dunton, whose best was good enough, even when I was too young and immature to realize it. To my **daughter**, Amari E. Forbes, who won't have to bare the strongholds from my past because I have reclaimed my life and DARED to LIVE!

CONTENTS

Tuere Dunton-Forbes

BUT FIRST...

Relinquish Control

I Dare U 2 Live" was initially a personal challenge to myself. One day, I was reflecting on how I had allowed my current life challenges to consume me too long, to the extent that it felt as though I was beginning to journey around the same mountain of defeat once again. My complete deliverance had not fully evolved, so I began to feel as though my "second wind" was only strong enough to help me *withstand* the storm, but not strong enough to get me through the storm. The fact that I was still battling many of the same onset physical and emotional symptoms from Fall of 2013 was enough evidence for me. I was becoming discouraged all over again and growing tired from the fight. I began to think of things that had improved in my life since the start of the storm. My marriage was strengthened; my understanding and reliance on God had increased; my ability to sleep was restored; I no longer suppressed my true feelings; I embraced transparency and was learning to relinquish control to God by accepting the things I could not control, because He could. As my list of blessings continued to grow, I realized that everything that I listed was a sign of LIFE! God had not allowed my challenges to result in my demise because all that was unraveling in my life was God's way of daring me to LIVE.

You see, 1st Corinthians 6:19-20 (TLB) reminds us that the Holy Spirit lives within each of us. God, our author owns all rights to our life (i.e., physical, spiritual, and mental). Our body is His! He bought us at the price of sacrificing His son. Therefore, we should use every part of our bodies, every situation we encounter to give glory back to God. It is because of Him that we still have LIFE to overcome, endure, conquer, withstand, witness and defeat. It is this birthright that spiritually tightened my bootstraps and prompted me to be intentional and become consistent with reclaiming what was rightfully mine—the right to live in WELLNESS.

Wellness is defined as a **life-long** process of moving towards optimal physical, intellectual, emotional, social, spiritual, occupational, financial, and environmental well-being. We each get to define what optimal looks like for our life based on the provision (access) God has already given us, the sacrifice (insurance) His son Jesus made for us, and the help (guidance and support) that Holy Spirit is readily available to render.

As the reader of this book, **I dare you** to relinquish all control over your life to the one who knew you before He formed you in the womb. Trust Him to guide your steps, never leave you or forsake you, see you through, fill your voids, organize a message out of your mess, heal what you nor the doctors can understand, and replace your weakness with His strength. He's **all**-knowing, **all**-powerful, and **ever**-present, so why not trust him to guide you today, tomorrow and through the unknown. **I DARE YOU TO LIVE!**

I DARE YOU TO LIVE...
AND SURRENDER

I am going to share with you every way God has challenged me to live with intention. When I first began writing this book, the chapters we ordered in reverse; however, I realized in order to effectively apply the nuggets I share throughout this book, you must first surrender. Surrendering was the greatest challenge, yet the most necessary lesson of them all. It had the greatest value and provided a solid foundation for the other challenges to manifest. Achievement in any area of your life requires a level of sacrifice. Surrendering your own will or desire to control your circumstances often presents as challenging because we normally (intentionally or unintentionally) take credit for the good things that happen in our lives, despite us not being the original author of our lives. I say it later again in the book, but I can't stress it enough. God is omniscient (He has infinite wisdom), omnipotent (He can do anything) and omnipresent (He is everywhere). What better G.P.S. (God Positioning System) to have while we navigate through this journey of life, than Holy Spirit? Yet, the only way to know how to access the G.P.S. is by first surrendering to Him.

As you are reading, you may find yourself wanting to go back or skip ahead to a particular chapter because the challenge covered in that chapter resonates with where you are in your journey, and that's quite all right. Just remember that for growth to truly manifest from the root, you must surrender.

Surrendering means making space in your life for God to work. Yes, God works in His own timing, but we can delay His timing by cluttering our lives with possessions and people that we value more than spending time with Him. Like anything else that grows, you too need room for the growth to occur in your life. Not sure what could be blocking God from working in your life? What do you spend most of your time doing? What consumes your thoughts the most? What do you invest most of your time, money, and energy in? Is it work? Is it material possessions? Is it a certain person or people? Are you chasing paper, power, or God's purpose for your life? Once you've answered the questions above, organize your answers in a list in the order of how much time, attention, and money you spend on each of them. This will give you a visual representation of what you value most in your life today.

Now ask yourself, "Is there room for God to work in my life?" Is He at the top of the list of what you value most? What will you do to begin surrendering your time and your life unto Him today? We want God to do immeasurable acts in our lives, but we limit the space that we give Him to work with. When surrendering, be willing to release all that you feel belongs to you unto Him. That which you need for your life's journey will remain and in some cases be multiplied. Whatever is necessary will be removed. Don't worry, our gracious God even knows and provides some of our wants too.

Psalm 25:4-10 (NKJV) Show me Your ways, O Lord; Teach me Your Paths. (MSG) Take me by the hand; Lead me down the path of truth. You are my Savior, aren't you? Mark the milestones of your mercy and love, God; Rebuild the ancient landmarks! Forget that I sowed wild oats; Mark me with your sign of love. Plan only the best for me, God! God is fair and just; He corrects the misdirected, Sends them in the right direction. He gives the rejects his hand,

And leads them step-by-step. From now on every road you travel Will take you to God. Follow the Covenant signs; Read the charted directions.

Your process to surrendering can be initiated just as the scriptures say. However, allow me to share my interpretation of each verse and how I applied them in my life to help you understand what has become a valuable lesson (that I sometimes must be retaught) of surrendering to God.

(Verse 4) "Show me Your ways, O Lord; Teach me Your Paths." (NKJV) When we surrender to something or someone it is because we have faith in its power. Having faith requires a relationship and being in a relationship requires two-way communication. Talk to God consistently; He doesn't require a specific form of communication. Would you expect your spouse or significant other to know you need them, or to remain in a relationship with you if you didn't communicate with them? Many of us begin the journey without first asking God if the destination we have set is the one He has prepared to receive us. When you ask God to show you His way, you must be willing to give Him your undivided attention. God's ways are always better than ours. They're not always the outcome we want, nor does He always reveal them in our timing but for someone who has already made the journey, I think it's best that we trust His way.

There are times when God will allow us to see our next destination, but He will lead us on a path that will take the destination out of our view. He does this to cause us to focus on His process. There's something more that He wants us to get out of the journey, than just getting to the destination. Sometimes, the shortest distance can be the fastest route to destruction. For example, your request may be for a generous sum of money to cancel debt. Your way may consist of working long hours and even adding a side hustle. God's way may consist of you drawing nigh to

Him so he can teach you how to better manage your finances and learn from your experiences, so you won't repeat them. God's way could also require you to open your hand in giving to others by helping them meet a need or by giving back to God (in faith) a portion of what He has blessed you with.

(Verse 5) "Take me by the hand; Lead me down the path of truth. You are my Savior, aren't you?" (MSG) In this verse, David is speaking to himself in reflection, reminding himself of who God is. Holy Spirit lives within each of us. To receive His guidance, we must first tune in and connect. My spiritual foundation was laid by the consistency of my mother's and grandmother's hands and hearts. They made sure I was in church regularly, taught me how to pray and memorize scriptures. Yet, it wasn't until my experience in "the pit" of grief, depression, pain, and the fear of the unknown that I learned how to really walk out in faith the power of applying God's word. My darkness was scary. Being in a place where you mentally begin to prepare yourself for death because living is too hard is not a good place to be.

One day during that time, my husband took the day off from work to stay home with me. After dropping my daughter off at daycare, he drove to the park near our house. He pulled up to the empty soccer field and sternly stated, "Get out!"

I responded, "And do what?"

"Go talk to God and tell Him how mad you are about everything that is going on in your life. He already knows it, but you need to say it. Go out into the middle of the field and scream, shout and whatever else you've been holding in."

I got out of the car and did just that. That release was what I needed at that moment. It was as if I was afraid to share my raw feelings with God. I was often trying to dress them up with praise and words of optimism, but the words couldn't take root until I completely released and surrendered. *"Whoever has your ear, has your future."* Be mindful of who you are listening to, even if it's you. It's okay to share our doubts with God. Just follow-up with...BUT I trust you.

(Verse 6) "Mark the milestones of your mercy and love, God; Rebuild the ancient landmarks!" As we receive instruction or guidance, we MUST take notes.

Write down what Holy Spirit is telling you. Trust His word and stand on it. The time we used to spend journaling or handcrafting tangible representations of visions was exchanged for swiping left, liking and pinning. However, there's research that suggests that our brains hold on to information better and longer when we write it down. This is because we activate our fine motor skills more when we use pen and paper than we do typing on a keyboard or tapping a screen. Making the time to write down our visions, what Holy Spirit downloads to us and putting them in a place where we can easily be reminded of the guidance increases the probability of us following through. When you are traveling through this life and wind up lost in unfamiliar territory, God continues to extend you His Grace and Mercy. God's word is always available in the premium version without any additional costs.

(Verse 7) "Forget that I sowed wild oats; Mark me with your sign of love. Plan only the best for me, God!" Youth is not always chronological; sometimes, it's spiritual. Here, David is saying, "God, I know I have not always acted as a child of God, but I need you to make me clean again so that when people see me, they see you. Please forgive my spiritual immaturity and my neglect to nurture our relationship the way it deserves to be nurtured. Restore me as the child of God you created me to be." Are you familiar with 1 Corinthians 13:11 *(When I was a child, I spoke as a child, I understood as a child, I thought as a child; but when I became a man, I put away childish things.)*? Throughout this journey of life, we must take time to purge ourselves of the things, people, and emotions that keep us from moving in the abundance that Christ died for. Some people must be dropped off or cut loose along the way. Every person, every behavior, and every belief is not meant to go to the next destination with you. Sometimes those who are meant to travel with you must first get left to realize that they missed the bus. There are things I had to put away for me to get to where I currently am in life: 1) unwillingness to commit, 2) other people's baggage, 3) fear of failing, and 4) doing what others did to fit in.

No, delay does not mean denial; however, when you allow others or things to delay you in moving in God's timing it can lead to drought. You won't have what you need to get to the next level, or to be who you need to be in that space. A good analogy for this part of the process is seeing the sign (while traveling on the highway) indicating that there's a gas station at the next exit, but you think to yourself or your traveling partner suggests, "Let's just wait until the next exit or until we arrive at the destination." This thought or suggestion is a result of your excitement to "just get there" that you want to shorten the process. Don't allow your focus on getting to the destination to distract you from heeding the lessons or necessary pauses along the process.

(Verse 8) "God is fair and just; He corrects the misdirected, Sends them in the right direction." God has already mapped out the road you will travel, but you must take the next step. God took the first step as He determined your destiny, now you just must take the next step in faith, believing what He has said about you. Constant communication with Holy Spirit ensures that you always have the right guidance. Just ask! It's okay when we don't know because God's strength is made perfect in our weaknesses. It reminds me of when my daughter is so determined to do things independent of my and my husband's help. Most times we'll let her try it if her safety is uncompromised. Often, she ends up coming to us for the same help we tried to offer her. God does us the same way when we think we can live independent of Him. He allows us to try, is there to receive us in love, and reminds us that life did not have to be as hard or as unfulfilling as we made it. He thought it was necessary for us to learn that from experience. God is not just the God of big trouble, low valleys, and diagnoses; He's also the God that can help us with the small decisions and challenges.

(Verse 9-10) "He gives the rejects his hand, And leads them step-by-step. From now on every road you travel Will take you to God. Follow the Covenant signs; Read the charted directions." By being distracted and allowing the distractions to take root in our lives, we qualify as "rejects." God is such an awesome and loving God that He gives us signs throughout our journeys in life to let us know when or if we're going in the right direction. If we don't pay attention to the signs and take time to study the instructions (God's word), we won't be able to understand what God is trying to tell us. Going through life without God's word is like trying to get instructions in a foreign country where you don't know the language, and you don't have a translator. Leaving us S-O-L (spiritually out of love). Don't drive through life distracted; it's a part of Satan's plan. As you're on this life's journey, rely on God's Positioning System to get you everywhere you need to go, regardless of the distance. When you are letting God tell you where to go, He incorporates rest stops in your journey, so you can be renewed and restored just enough to continue to the next destination. Surrender to His guidance.

Isaiah 40: 30-31 (NKJV) *Even the youths shall faint and be weary, And the young men shall utterly fall, But those who wait on the Lord Shall renew their strength; They shall mount up with wings like eagles, They shall run and not be weary, They shall walk and not faint.*

Gratefully arrive. Say "thank you" as it's a form of praise! When you finally get to your destination, don't forget to acknowledge that you could have not withstood the distractions or overcame the challenges without God's guidance and His positioning. Or, for many of us, His repositioning. Each of us were born with an innate well within, designed to be filled with true contentment (your high-octane gas), which can only be gained through the love of God. To love Him, you must know something about Him. You can't fill up on the love of God if you are not speaking to Him, listening to Him, taking notes, documenting the things He is telling you, purging the baggage, stepping out in faith, and believing and reading the signs.

* * *

Question to Ponder:
Now that I have dared you to surrender, what's your next step?

_____

_____

_____

_____

_____

_____

_____

_____

_____

_____

"Everything you need, God already is."
—PRISCILLA SHIRER

I DARE YOU TO LIVE...
AND BELIEVE

To those encountering an experience with traumatic grief for the first time: what you knew as normal is forever changed. That feeling of being trapped in the bubble of grief while everyone else continues to live is a feeling that is uncomfortable and suffocating, yet real! Take it one day at a time, and whatever emotion you are experiencing, express it. Please, don't suppress your emotions; the grief cycle doesn't always happen in a particular order. Draw near to God in a way you have never done before. Lean on your support system and your inner circle. They want you to. Hang up whatever capes (i.e., Superwoman or Superman, The Resilient One, or The Go to Person, etc.) you've worn before your loss. It's your time to receive from others. Take advantage of counseling opportunities (i.e., church, Employee Assistance Program (E.A.P.) through your employer, or community-based). Talking about how you truly feel will hurt at first, but it will eventually become a path of healing. God NEVER wastes a hurt!

It was by faith that I've been able to find joy along this journey of mourning. Although I know that God never intended for us to live eternally on this earth, I struggled with how a God who's so good could allow my father to be physically defeated by a disease that He has healed others from. My father retired three months before he died; however, he didn't have the opportunity to enjoy all the benefits of retirement like traveling, spending more time with those he loved, picking up additional hobbies, and spending more time landscaping his yard. My mother died without a plan for retirement. After she was fired from a job she had invested years in, she cashed in her 401K to make ends meet with hopes of finding another "permanent" job. That didn't occur before she took her last breath at the age of sixty, just five weeks shy of her 61st birthday. As I long for their presence, I'm reminded that though they were mine for 35 and 38 years, they ultimately both belonged to God first, as He is our first love. The term of His loan of them to me ended. Now it is my responsibility to use the love, wisdom, and memories that they each sowed into my life as fuel to empower me throughout my new assignment of "Empowering Others to Live as the C.E.O.s of Their Health."

My pain has evolved into my purpose as God has not wasted my hurts. He is healing me while making clearer His purpose for my life. He can do the same for you if you allow Him to walk with you; lean into His process and believe in His power, which is greater than yours. Your belief in His power must become the foundation of the work He does in and through you.

Knowing God is everywhere, knows all things and can do all things is a no brainer for me. However, I have found myself, on more than one occasion, wondering if God would do for me what I have witnessed him do for countless others. Faith, like Grace and Mercy, is a gift from God, readily available to us by reading and hearing His word, communicating with Him (forming a relationship), and then deciding to believe what the word says.

Belief is a choice. It is the attitude we take that something is true. To believe in something or someone is to have faith in that person or thing. My moments of unbelief have often resulted from my lack of faith in my worthiness and/or God's timing. It creeps in when there is a time lapse in the renewing of my mind, when I've become consumed with distractions including my inner chatterbox or when I'm measuring myself with someone else's stick. In addition to influence from distractions, unbelief can also be the by-product of self-inflicted standards that we struggle to reach. The standards that we set for ourselves can sometimes cause us to focus more on what we are not instead of what we are. Or, on the other hand, on what we don't want to become or remain. We become so focused on achieving the image we have created in our minds that we don't nurture who we are, right where we are.

Nurturing who we are helps us to believe in ourselves. It's easier for us to doubt than believe because to believe in ourselves, someone, or something, we must first have a relationship with that which we want to believe in. For this to occur, we must take the attitude that who we are in the moment is true, and the current truth can change based on our decisions. Developing or nurturing a relationship ensures there's an active connection. This connection allows for us to develop a level of faith. Faith in the seen, the process and the unseen. This connection can be weakened or blocked by various distractions we encounter. How we respond to these distractions can either weaken or strengthen the relationship. If the relationship is weakened, your level of faith will also be negatively impacted. To strengthen your belief in yourself or God you must:

- Invest quality time in getting to know yourself! Who we are changes with time and life experiences. For example, I am a planner. I like to have a plan for just about everything (I'll talk more about this later in the book). Planning helps me stay organized and helps things run smoother in my life. However, ever since I've added additional people to my immediate family (husband and daughter), my plans don't always unfold as smoothly as I would like them to. This is because my plans are often affected by the attitudes and behaviors of two other people who have their own opinion and ideas.

My plans had always worked for me; well at least 90% of the time. So, it was hard for me to understand why it would be hard for them to follow them exactly how *I* drafted them. Sometimes, this caused delays or newly drafted plans, causing me to question myself or doubt my ability to accomplish what *I* set out to do. I had to accept that the changes in my life were requiring me to change. It took many prayers, listening, and willingness to accepts God's guidance, whether directly communicated or conveyed through others. I didn't have to stop planning, just change how I planned, and be more considerate of their interests and style of thinking. Over time, I've adjusted; however, there are still times when I will measure my recent accomplishments against the way I used to be able to accomplish goals as the single, independent, childless Tuere. But that's not who I am anymore. I now give myself more grace. I know I am just as, if not more, capable of accomplishing what I go after as wife and a mother as I did solo.

- Affirm your goals with your words! Write them on your mirror, on index cards and post them on your wall, or record yourself saying what you will have as if you already have it. Recite your words or listen to them frequently, until they come to fruition.

My mother used to always tell me, "Closed mouths don't get fed." She would especially remind me of this when I was hesitant to ask my father for additional financial support (from fear that he would say he couldn't do more than what he was currently doing). She would bring it up when I was reluctant to try something new or speak up for myself. She'd say, "Pray about it first, believe it is happening, then go for it."

Yes, my daddy's answer would mostly likely be as I predicted; however, I still managed to get what I needed. What I didn't realize then was that by verbalizing it through prayers and with affirmation, it allowed my words to take root in the earth. It did not always manifest exactly the way I imagined, but it was always exactly what I needed. Our words are powerful, and that's why we must choose them carefully. Just as God created things by speaking them as though they were, we have that same power within us because His Spirit lives within us. We must live as though we know that we know what we know. And that's that we have the power to speak life into our goals and circumstances. Even today, I see a difference in my level of belief and the results when I constantly speak over an idea, goal, or desire versus when I harbor it as only an internal thought. Words make a difference. Patrice Washington says it like this: "What you verbalize, you magnify and magnetize!"

- Trust the process! Just like most things we desire to have, believing in yourself or God is not an instant achievement, it's a process. The Oxford Dictionary defines *process* as *"a series of _actions or steps_ taken _in order_ to achieve a _particular end._"* We often want the _particular end_, but don't want to adhere to _the actions or steps_ in the _order_ they were intended to be completed in. When we don't know the order, we often won't seek wise counsel to help us figure it out. Operating out of order promotes delay. Delay in us strengthening our belief, delay in us understanding the process and delay in us achieving our *particular end*. Take me authoring this book for example. The vision came to me in 2015. It has taken me six years to complete because I struggled with staying committed to the process. A process that has included:

1. Making time to write (i.e., journaling, keeping notes in my phone, jotting on sticky notes, etc.)...and moving past my excuses

2. Reading and studying God's word to understand what I was supposed to learn from my experiences...and moving past my excuses

3. Being vulnerable and transparent about my experiences, not just with God, but with others (I talk more about this later in the book)...and moving past my excuses

4. Praying often, making sacrifices...and moving past my excuses

5. Consulting with more than one, and then hiring a writing coach...and moving past my excuses

6. Developing a plan, budgeting, honoring deadlines...and yep, you got it--**MOVING PAST MY EXCUSES!**

It has been a process! One that has stretched me beyond my comfort zone while causing me to declutter my mind and my life, so that God could work "exceedingly abundantly above all that I could imagine according to His power that works in me." If I just believe...

* * *

Question to Ponder:
Where is belief the greatest challenge in your life?

_____

_____

_____

_____

_____

_____

_____

_____

_____

_____

_____

_____

_____

_____

_____

_____

_____

_____

_____

"Don't allow your disbelief to cause you to miss out on the rest that was promised to you. The proof is in His word."
—CHOSEN

I DARE YOU TO LIVE... AND FORGIVE

orgiveness is more beneficial to the giver than the receiver. Extending forgiveness allows you to free up space in your heart, your mind, and your body. In your heart, by allowing you to release the tension and stress created from harboring the offense. In your mind, by allowing you to make room for mental creativity and clarity. In your body, by allowing you to release the tension that blocks healing and creativity.

I've always loved hard when I've connected with those I perceived to be "good people." My loving hard also came with the expectation that the one receiving my love would never do anything to hurt me.

Forgiveness doesn't automatically equal a renewed relationship, but it does release the strain. I know this may seem unrealistic to some because all humans make mistakes that in many cases hurt someone connected to them. These mistakes can become life lessons to those who made them and those impacted. When forgiveness is not extended, the unforgiveness turns into negative energy and is often projected in the decisions we make, the company we keep, and our expectations of the universe.

My first experience with deep-rooted unforgiveness was when I learned that all my siblings on my father's side had the one thing in common that I longed for. They all had the "intact family" experience with our father living under the same roof. My mother and father were never married. Yes, I am the result of an out-of-wedlock conception. Based on the details of both sides of the story, my father was *in wedlock* just not with *my* mother. My chance of having an "intact family" experience shattered before I even saw daylight. It was not until my late elementary school years that I began to see myself as the black sheep of all my father's four children. Surely there was something I did wrong to rob myself of the opportunity to wake up and come home to my father living under the same roof. I often thought, *"My brothers and sister all experienced it, so why not me?"* My unrest and questions caused my mother to reveal the truth behind my existence. Although my father regularly sent an agreed amount of child support, it was difficult for him to be in two places at one time. Therefore, his physical distance ignited resentment.

I once heard that living in unforgiveness is like drinking poison and expecting the other person to die. I can relate to this as I used to be one who held grudges without an expiration date. It wasn't until my mid-thirties that I realized the benefit of forgiveness is not for those who hurt or disappointed me; it's for me. Even when the hurt was self-inflicted, I had to forgive myself. Refusing to forgive causes you to carry the emotional pain of what occurred. Not forgiving will not change what occurred, nor does it guarantee that it won't happen again by the same person or someone different. It's the lesson you learn from the situation, including the forgiveness, which helps you heal.

In 2012, shortly after my daughter turned one, I became emotionally weighted. The weight became so overwhelming that I decided to reach out to a therapist. During my sessions with the therapist, she helped me understand that the weight I was carrying was not just from the new roles of mother and wife that I had acquired in the last five years; the weight also consisted of unresolved issues that I had experienced throughout my life. Yes, being a parent and a spouse can, at times, be overwhelmingly heavy, but when you add that to years of unforgiveness, it makes the most recent roles seem downright unbearable. I was carrying **unforgiveness** for being inappropriately touched as a child by a relative who was also a child and for mimicking that behavior towards other children during my childhood. I was carrying the **unforgiveness** of my parents for not being able to afford to send me to college; thus, resulting in me having to take out student loans that I am still paying back. I was carrying **unforgiveness** towards myself for withdrawing from a doctoral program in 2004 (even though I knew it was the BEST decision for me), because I thought that just maybe I may be better off financially had I stuck with it. I was carrying **unforgiveness** towards myself for being in an extended relationship with a married man during my single post-secondary days, and though I had repented for that sin years ago, I thought possibly that was the reason my husband and I could not see eye-to-eye on several things in our relationship. I was carrying **unforgiveness** towards a relative for a financial wedge created between him and my mother. I was carrying **unforgiveness** towards my mom's ex-husband for his role in their domestically violent relationship.

Whew, just sharing this makes me wonder how I had room in my life to pursue a career, become a wife and then a mother while carrying all this around. Unfortunately, that is what many of us do. We cover up what makes us uncomfortable with something new and when that something new presents a challenge, we put something else on top of it because covering it is easier than doing the work of forgiving.

True forgiveness requires you to first acknowledge that something occurred that resulted in your offense, hurt, embarrassment, or disappointment. If you don't acknowledge the root of the unforgiveness it will manifest in other ways leading to anger, resentment, and bitterness toward the offender. In some cases, this may cause those you love and care about to become casualties of the unaddressed emotions. I once heard Pastor Michael Todd (Transformation Church in Tulsa, OK) define forgiveness as "the **intentional** and **voluntary** process by which a victim undergoes a change in feelings and attitude regarding an offense and overcomes negative emotions such as resentment and vengeance." This definition is so accurate for me. That's exactly what I had to do. Peel back the layers to get to the root of my unforgiveness and be willing to do the work—whatever that looked like to achieve forgiveness. My work had to be intentional, and an elective decision made by me.

Layer by layer, I began doing the work. I began first by having a conversation with my husband about feeling overwhelmed with my various roles and responsibilities, where I could use more support from him, and how he could extend the support. As time progressed, I also shared with him details about the deeper work I needed to do on my unresolved issues from the past. Sharing these details with him was key because I would also need his support as I swept all the suppressed emotions from under the rug. After praying for additional strength, I began making calls to those I could to initiate the difficult conversations. Although the conversations were uncomfortable, to say the least, it was evident that weight lifted from them as well as for me. This release allowed me to continue the work from within. Forgiveness is freeing and freedom. Embracing the process of forgiveness, and then extending forgiveness to the others releases them from the debt left behind from the offense. Not only that, it makes room in your life for emotional and spiritual development.

* * *

Questions to Ponder:
How do you address unforgiveness?
Who do you need to forgive?
Who do you need to ask for forgiveness?

_____
_____
_____
_____
_____
_____
_____
_____
_____
_____
_____
_____
_____
_____
_____
_____
_____
_____

*"Unforgiveness chains us to the past, poisons
the present and keeps us from what the
Lord has for the future."*
—UNKNOWN

I DARE YOU TO LIVE...
AND BE TRANSPARENT

Growing up, my mother used to tell my brother and I that, "What goes on in our house, stays in our house!" This was her way of reminding us that it was not our family's business that she continued to keep company with a man who initiated domestic violent rages at times. Although her demand did not stop us from confiding in certain relatives we trusted, it did set the tone for my life, and how I have managed challenging moments. When life became overwhelming, I would seclude myself from most until the storm passed. That was exactly what I tried to do after my dad passed away. The depression from the grief, and from the onset of the symptoms from what I later learned was Lyme Disease were beating me down.

Putting parenting and being a wife on pause was not an option, so I pressed through in the best way I knew how. I hid in closets and bathrooms throughout my house to cry, and ask God "why" and "what"? There were many days when I pulled the shade over my office window to weep from the overwhelming feeling of full body pulsating, and the burning sensation that encompassed my body whenever I made contact with any piece of furniture (i.e., bed, chair, etc.). The compression against my skin felt as if someone had doused me in gasoline and lit a match. The broken record of hearing medical specialist after specialist say, "It's anxiety and grief! You're not allowing yourself to grieve," only heightened the anxiety more than it soothed it. I clearly understood that grieving was a process. I am a professional counselor by training, but I knew there was something more at the root of my symptoms. Something that another recommended prescription was not going to fix.

On the outside, I looked normal to those who knew me or read my medical records, which indicated anemic, occasional sinus infections and normal ranges of everything checked during my annual visits. However, on the inside there was a major war going on. One without an understood cause. One that was reaping havoc on every biological system necessary to live a healthy and happy life. I did not know what to do, and Dr. Google was only making things worse. According to my searches, I could have multiple sclerosis (MS), preliminary stages of amyotrophic lateral sclerosis (ALS), or fibromyalgia just to name a few. No disrespect to anyone living with these diseases, but the information I read created fear to an extent that led to me mentally planning my demise. My weeping was no longer just from the pain I felt, but now included: 1) the fear of the unknown, 2) the visions of not being present with my family anymore, and 3) the reality that we could not afford to commit to the additional tests and medications that were suggested to confirm or to treat their "educated guesses."

The pain and discomfort became unbearable. So much so that on July 2nd, 2014, after dropping my daughter off at daycare, I prayed for God to end my sorrow and let me die by allowing my car to run into the nearest pole. I was not bold enough to do it, so he would have to be the driving force behind it. His response was, "Tuere I am getting ready to elevate you to a level where you will be empowering many, but you must stay in this moment as preparation. How are you going to empower and encourage others out of pits, through valleys and over mountains if you don't know what it feels like to be in those types of situations?" That intimate moment with Holy Spirit confirmed that my current circumstances were not going to be my forever if I trusted His process and stopped expecting Him to operate within my expectations. This encounter helped me shift my focus from healing to increasing my understanding of how God could use my mess for His message.

From early childhood to my teen years, I was very slender. So much so, that one of my aunts used to lovingly call me "Skinny Mini" and "Olive Oil" after the female character in the cartoon *Popeye*. I used to giggle or sometimes laugh whenever she called me that. Unbeknownst to me at the time, the nickname negatively affected my self-esteem and my perception of what I thought I should look like to be considered attractive, as "Olive Oil" was not an attractive character. Deep inside, I was embarrassed because that name was a reminder that my physical development (breasts, hips, and butt) was delayed in comparison to my female cousins who were close to my age and many of my friends and peers. I wanted to fit in with what I thought was necessary and so I did what I thought I needed to do to speed up the process or at least make me look more mature than I was. During the early 90's, there were rumors that rubbing butter, yes butter, on your chest would help your breast grow. Yep, I tried it! It was a failed attempt.

There was also this notion that having sex at an early age helped your hips spread and would ensure your boyfriend's faithfulness to you. Yep, thirteen was my number, and that failed too. I roll my eyes at the thought of being so naïve and gullible, but it is my truth. Knowing what I know now, I surely would have waited until I was married to have sex. Abstaining until marriage would have spared me the emotional distress that comes along with lust and mistaking physical and emotional attraction for true love. It would have also prevented me from making additional decisions that I later regretted (i.e., starting birth control pills at age 16 and staying on them until I was 35). It wasn't until adulthood that I fully understood why sex wasn't intended to be a frivolous act, but one enjoyed between a husband and his wife. It is intended to strengthen the bond of marriage, and each time we engage in sex our body interprets it as though we are engaging with the one we are bonded to in holy matrimony. There's a certain level of maturity, commitment and responsibility that comes with sex, a level I had not achieved at the age of thirteen.

I thought going to college and getting married were two ways to guarantee that I would not have to live the common lifestyle of "check-to-check." However, I now know it's not the accomplishment of these noteworthy milestones that guarantees success; it is the relationship with God that helps you navigate the challenges of life in a more efficient way. His word in Hebrews 13:5 (NKJV) tells us to "be content with what we have. For God Himself said he will never leave us nor forsake us." Being a child of God doesn't guarantee that we won't be pressured, tempted, or challenged; it guarantees that we have guidance through His word and that we are never alone.

Earning a college degree made me more marketable in the world of employment, allowing me to secure a salaried position with health benefits, but it has been God's guidance that has allowed me to grow within my career field through increased knowledge, wisdom, discernment, and self-discipline. While getting married did increase my household income, it is the commitment of doing the work to stay married with God's guidance that has sustained our union. Being transparent takes a lot of courage! It causes you to be authentic, first with yourself then with those who you are led to share with. Transparency means you are putting your truth before others' judgement. Any fear that may arise from an unknown response falls second to the level of respect you develop for yourself from accepting and loving yourself right where you are. It's that level of respect that has allowed me to get comfortable with owning the truths I have shared with you. No longer am I held in spiritual bondage as a result of feeling like I had to keep my truth a secret. No, I am not parading my business down "front street," but I am no longer living in fear, with a side of anxiety. My transparency has created room for growth and possibilities. It has also allowed me to extend support to those who can relate because they trust the experience I have gained through embracing my truth. Each of the experiences I have shared are a part of my life's story, not my conclusion.

* * *

Questions to Ponder:
Is there anything or anyone keeping you
from progressing in life?
How is this impacting your life?
What are the positive benefits of you
addressing these strongholds?

_____

_____

_____

_____

_____

_____

_____

_____

"Brokenness = Openness"
—CHOSEN

I DARE YOU TO LIVE...
WITHOUT BOUNDARIES

Attending college out of state was not only my opportunity to enhance my knowledge of my chosen area of study, but it was also my escape from a life impacted by others' dysfunction and substance abuse and my bridge to life as I know it now filled with healthier relationships, gifts beyond measure and strength I didn't know I had. So many of us allow ourselves to become confined to our limitations and comfort zones. We will invest more time and energy creating comfort within our limits than we do pushing past them. We've learned how to function within the mental and spiritual confinements that stunt our progress in life. We trick ourselves into believing that it's easier to redecorate the invisible walls that hold us back, than it would be to knock them down or climb over them to see what's on the other side. You must release yourself from negative limits and unhealthy labels. Learn how to love yourself right where you are and nourish your life to promote growth and longevity.

Based on my bloodline, living check-to-check, being a mother out of wedlock, and working a job for financial stability instead of financial freedom and emotional growth are all a part of my lineage. As children, many of us set our future aspirations based on achieving career goals that appeared to guarantee financial security.

What we were blinded to was the need to first focus on being the change we want to see by breaking generational curses, knocking down barriers and climbing over or walking around our emotional and spiritual mountains. There were several labels and limits I contested because of my circumstances and the environment I grew up in. For example, I remember processing that I was my father's only child who didn't grow up with him waking up next to my mother or being in the same home for dinner. I never experienced him asking me, "How was school today?" Putting this into perspective resulted in me feeling like an outcast or the black sheep of his litter. I questioned my worthiness and wondered why my story couldn't include more "remember when's" with my father and I under the same roof. The distant physical presence of my father, plus my mother's short-lived relationship with my youngest brother's father (so short that I don't remember them ever living together, although they did), and her domestically violent relationship with her ex-husband, all influenced how I approached relationships with males in my life from middle school on. I did not have consistent, positive examples of women having healthy relationships with men.

My mother was one of eight biological daughters (nine raised in the home), and my grandfather was in the military, causing him to be away from home a lot. I don't have any memories of my maternal grandparents cultivating a life together. They both were present and active in my life, but my memories of my grandfather include him having a separate residence from my grandmother before he suffered a stroke and had to move into a rehabilitation center. Later, he resided in a retirement center for the elderly who could not care for themselves. Out of all my grandmother's daughters, I only recall two of them having what I thought were healthy relationships with men beyond five years.

This lack of exposure to healthy lasting relationships with the other sex caused me to crave what I didn't see. I knew that I wanted them to be in my life, but I did not know what the process should look like through a healthy lens, or that it was truly okay for me to focus on just being by myself and being okay with it. It is unhealthy limits and labels like these that become the blueprint that we follow to create our future. I used my opportunity to attend college out of state as an exposure gateway to something different. The relationships I developed throughout my matriculation allowed me to see more positive, real-life examples of healthy relationships. Visiting the states, cities and homes of my college friends opened my eyes to off-set examples of Bill and Claire Huxtable, Phil and Viv Banks, George and Louise Jefferson, and Carl and Harriette Laura Winslow. It also helped me to value even more extrafamilial relationships that were built on trust, respect, acceptance, and love. It was through these experiences that I realized that "home" could be established wherever my heart lied, and I did not have to return to the land of Hotlanta for it to continue to hold value in my life.

If you are a fan of the hit series *Empire,* then you may recall in the first season when Lucious (Terrence Howard) was first diagnosed with ALS (Amyotrophic Lateral Sclerosis) and how he began to plan for the worst-case scenario. He invested most of his energy in determining which of his son's would take over the company and maximizing every business opportunity, while destroying anyone who got in his way. Not once did we see him ask God for guidance or understanding. Lucious never reflected on what aspects of his lifestyle may have triggered his symptoms, nor how he wanted to use his projected remaining lifespan to positively impact the lives of others. Take a moment to imagine you received a report of detriment (i.e., diagnoses, foreclosure, repossession, death of a close loved one etc.). What would be your response? Many of us would feel like the wind had been knocked out of us. Now, imagine receiving a second lease on life from that detrimental situation. In episode eleven, Lucious received his second wind when he was told he was misdiagnosed. He became empowered when the label was stripped away. This scene reminded me of my responses throughout life to various challenges and uncomfortable situations that created limitations or formed into invisible labels that were either affixed upon me by others or myself and how I felt when I realized that I was not what I feared or regretted. Our limits and labels are only a part of our story and not the ending. The adversary uses what we fear, are ashamed of and what we regret as weapons of intimidation.

Now let me bring your attention to 1st Peter 5:6-10 (NKJV): *Therefore humble yourselves under the mighty hand of God, that He may exalt you in due time, casting all your care upon Him, for He cares for you. Be sober, be vigilant; because your adversary the devil walks about like a roaring lion, seeking whom he may devour. Resist him, steadfast in the faith, knowing that the same sufferings are experienced by your brotherhood in the world. But may the God of all grace, who called us to His eternal glory by Christ Jesus, after you have suffered a while, perfect, establish, strengthen, and settle you.*

Verse six is telling us to STOP. Take a break from trying to have the answer to every problem. Stop expecting "you" to have the solution or to know the reason behind the circumstance. Take the expectation off you and give it to God, the omniscient one! The most common immediate response to unexpected news is to try to find a resolution. Some of us will go the extra step to understand the why and how with hopes of preventing manifestation of it, but the most common response is, "What can "I" do to fix this?"

Verse seven is instructing us to cast—throw forcefully in a specified direction—that which is laden upon us. God wants us to cast ALL our cares upon Him, never to be retrieved again. That includes the labels we have placed on ourselves and our circumstances (i.e., situations, people). Casting takes effort, and in most cases is not a one-time deal. It's repetitive until your faith catches up with your effort. Casting strengthens your faith muscles. You must cast until you get your peace. Whenever we feel depleted, threatened, defeated, or overwhelmed, our first response should be to give it to God. He is the author of each of our journeys.

Verse eight tells us how to show up. To become "sober" and "vigilant" we need to focus on Christ; meditate on His word! His word renews our mind, restores our spirit, and prepares us to withstand what lies ahead. Satan, the adversary, does not have the authority to harm you, but he does have the ability to distract you (remember Job) with his roaring. What does the roaring look/sound/feel like in your life? Is it...

- The ache/physical pain?
- The unexpected/high bill?
- Finding out about your spouse's infidelity?
- That disobedient child?
- That not so good evaluation at work?

God allows Satan to roar with the expectation that we will jump towards Him. Unfortunately, many of us flee in the opposite direction, which puts us further away from the guidance we need, and God's peace in the process. It is after we become sober and vigilant that we can, with conviction, do as Verse 9 instructs us to do. Tell Satan how big your God is! Constantly speak God's word to your situation. You are not the first, nor the only one to encounter and endure a situation of this magnitude, and neither will you be the last. As you draw nigh to God, also draw nigh to those who He has strategically placed around you for such a time as this. God never intended for us to be alone. Hebrews 10:25 instructs us to, **"Not forsaking the assembling of ourselves together, as is the manner of some; but exhorting (strongly encouraging) one**

another: and so much the more, as ye see the day approaching."
(NKJV) It is vital that we surround ourselves with people who look
like what we are working to achieve, people who bless you with
their transparency, and those who will point us back towards God's
unchanging hand when we get distracted. If you have yet to find
those people, speak them into existence by reciting God's word.
Here are four scriptures that have helped me discern who these
people are in my life:

- *"Do not be anxious about anything, but in every situation, by
  prayer and petition, with thanksgiving, present your requests to
  God."-**Philippians 4:6***
- *"I have told you these things, so that in me you may have peace. In
  this world you will have trouble. But take heart! I have overcome
  the world."-**John 16:33 (NIV)***
- *"Let us not become weary in doing good, for at the proper time we
  will reap a harvest if we do not give up."-**Galatians 6:9 (NIV)***
- *"Ye are of God, little children, and have overcome them: because
  greater is he that is in you, than he that is in the world."*
  *-**John 4:4 (KJV)***

The pain, suffering or fear of the unknown can be so
overwhelming that it causes us to yearn for the product over the
process. In Verse 10, you are reminded that the God who loves you
so much sacrificed His son for you to guarantee you eternal glory.
This is the same God who:

- Can transition you to where you want to be.
- Has and will continue to provide your every need.
- Gives you things you haven't earned.

His presence is more precious than the external circumstances or
labels that we thought were permanent. The only permanent label
we should wear is Child of God! God has grace. **His opinion of you**

will never change. He wants you to be impacted by Him. Remember, when Christ died for our sins He carried the labels that others had placed on Him to the cross:

- False Prophet
- Thief
- Traitor
- Impostor

He bore the burden of being negatively labeled so you don't have to. Child of God, now is the time for you to strip yourself of those heavy-laden labels that have hindered you from walking in your true identity. Receive the label that God placed on you before He formed you in the womb!

Remember...

- You are BLESSED!
- You are SAVED!
- You are HEALED!
- You are FAVORED!

All the amenities of being a CHILD OF GOD!

* * *

Question to Ponder:
What labels and limits have mentally, spiritually,
or physically imprisoned your progress?

_____

_____

_____

_____

_____

"Don't limit your challenges, challenge your limits."
—UNKNOWN

I DARE YOU TO LIVE...
AND BREATHE & REST

"Take a deep breath, in your nose and out of your mouth." I recall the paramedics saying this when I had my first experience with hyperventilation because of competing in my middle school's track and field event. That had never happened before (both me participating in an official race and me losing control of my breath). I was excited about competing, yet anxious about not losing. I thought I was dying! The school called my Mama at work, and she flew over in her "Stankin Lankin" (Lincoln Town Car). She was overwhelmed with concern as she too knew this had never happened before. They had me breathing inside a brown paper bag to help me regain control. Finally, the paramedic explained that the excitement from the competition resulted in me holding my breath while running instead of properly breathing, which caused hyperventilation (breathing at an abnormally rapid rate, thus limiting the amount of carbon dioxide exhaled while breathing in oxygen). This improper way of breathing is what many of us engage in when we encounter fear, excessively worry, become overly anxious about something, overexert ourselves or panic. Although this was my first experience with hyperventilating, it was not my last.

As a teenager and young adult, it mostly occurred when I engaged in some form of physical competition (i.e., hi-stepping, step team, etc.). As an adult it resurfaced with the unexpected deaths of my parents and during my initial symptoms of Lyme Disease. You may be thinking, *"I don't hyperventilate when I experience those emotions."* That is great if you do not. What I have found to be the common denominators of it all are anxiety and fear. I am not trying to teach you how to prevent hyperventilation. What I want you to glean from this chapter is how to healthily respond to the situations that can trigger warning signs that you need to breathe, and that your mind and body needs rest.

Let's talk about FEAR (False Evidence Appearing Real). It is the emotion we experience due to negative narratives we tell ourselves. The narrative may consist of some facts, but it is nicely wrapped up in the unknown. For example, "I lost my father to Stage 4 Lung Cancer in 2013. *(Fact)* He was diagnosed on October 18, 2013, and took his last breath on October 31, 2013, at 5:47 p.m. *(Fact)* We were initially told that he had bronchitis; then it changed to pneumonia and was eventually confirmed as cancer. No one could have told me in July of that year, when he retired from his job of 40+ years, that he would be gone in four months. Yet, the domino effect led to his demise and left his children with unanswered questions and a mound of anxiety. *(Fact)* As I dizzily moved through the stages of grief, I began to rationalize that every physical discomfort I experienced (headache, pinched nerve, tingle, etc.) must have been a sign that I too was headed to the dark tunnel of cancer. *(My Negative Narrative)*

The Truth...

- My father was an avid smoker all my life and most of his.
- My physical symptoms were the onset of my then undiagnosed Lyme Disease that was exacerbated by my grief.

- What I was feeling was real. My life had become encapsulated in a bubble while the rest of the world continued to move on.
- My mental and physical health needed support, but I was not dying from cancer like my daddy.

Fear and negative self-talk spiritually paralyzes you and shackles your emotions. My perception changed when my narrative changed, and my narrative changed when I began studying God's word beyond Sunday service and regularly speaking it over my situation. Once I began speaking His word over my situation, it shifted from my hands to God's hands, releasing the stronghold on my thoughts and freeing my mind up to see God's hand working in my situation.

Self-care starts with the first word of this sentence. As I am writing this part of the chapter, I'm on a flight back from a much-needed getaway with some F.R.I.S.T.A.s (Friends-Representing-Infinite-Sisterhood-Through it-All) and acquaintances. These fristas have been connected to my life since my undergraduate years of study, and since that time forward it is revealed increasingly what a blessing they are to my family and me. I value times like this because being in their presence reiterates the importance of being available to nurture the connection you have with those who hold value in your life: God, family, fristas, friends and most importantly, myself. Please understand that I am in no way placing myself at a greater value than God, for without Him I could not and would not be. What I am saying is that you must make time to get to know yourself to understand who you were created to be. The more intentional I am about making time to understand and accept who I truly am, the more I understand who God is in me and who God created me to be. I've gained more clarity about those connected to my life, my role in their life and their role in my life. This clarity has allowed me to see the bonds that need to be nurtured, those that have been strengthened and the reason behind those that have been or need to be severed. Taking this time away allowed me to breathe.

There are times when life's expectations, whether self-imposed or projected, can cause you to experience stress-related suffocation in the natural or in the spirit. This spiritual suffocation can manifest in symptoms of anxiety, joint pain, gastrointestinal issues, hormonal imbalance, skin reactions, migraines, hyperventilation, night trimmers and so much more. I once heard someone describe negative feelings as "emotions looking for a resolution." Until we are available to understand and effectively address those feelings in their truth, they will continue to seek out a resolve. Failure to get to the root cause can result in a depleted temple or disease.

You deserve to make yourself a priority in your life. Wise investments yield great returns, not just for you, but in most cases for those connected to you as well. Making time to rest (Remove-Emotional-Stress & Trust God), whether active or complete, is an investment in your life. Today's society and social media implies that to "win" in life we must have a page on every platform, be current in the latest fashion trends, have access to the popular social events and have a certain amount in our bank account. So many of us are working to acquire all of this on top of the other hats we wear (i.e., parent, spouse, business owner, employee, friend, caretaker, etc.) It can be overwhelming at times! Especially when we are so focused on doing, checking items off our to-do lists, being what others need us to be for them, and not being fully present first with ourselves and with our higher source, or allowing time to be replenished. I know, I know, it sounds cliché-ish, but it is so true, you cannot pour from an empty cup. Even God made time to rest after He created the earth (Genesis 2:2) and made it a weekly commandment. He rested before feeding the five thousand (Matthew 14;13), and then again before walking on the sea to calm down His disciples (Matthew 14:23). So, if the Alpha and Omega needed rest in all His doing, what makes the ones He created any different?

He is so amazing! He knew we would get distracted with doing too much and not setting aside time to restore that He included several reminders throughout His word in the Bible. But, if we are not intentional about getting in His word on a regular basis to hear His voice and guidance, or if we keep company with people who don't have that habit either, how can we be reminded of the importance of resting? It is God's word that reminds us that any challenges we are experiencing are not new, and there is a way to gain peace during it all. It is through rest and through His word. You do not have to memorize the Bible. Start by finding a scripture or two that speaks to not only to your circumstances, but also to your heart. I'll share three that have given me peace in the time of unrest:

- *"Don't become so well-adjusted to your culture that you fit into it without even thinking. Instead, fix your attention on God. You'll be changed from the inside out."* - **Romans 12:2 (MSG)**
- *"Therefore, we do not become discouraged [spiritless, disappointed or afraid]. Though our outer self is wasting away, yet our inner self is being [progressively] renewed day by day."* - **2 Corinthians 4:16 (AMP)**
- *"Do not be anxious about anything, but in every situation, by prayer and petition, with thanksgiving, present your requests to God. And the peace of God, which transcends all understanding, will guard your hearts and your minds in Christ Jesus."* - **Philippians 4:6-7 (TLV)**

Many think rest doesn't come until retirement or when they achieve a specific title or a certain figure in their bank account. Rest is necessary for self-care. You must own your need to press pause when needed. Consistently incorporating moments of rest (complete or active) helps you regain or maintain control of your present and future. Meditation is a simple, yet effective skill that can help you incorporate moments of rest. Meditation is the act of reflecting in thought. Many people practice meditation by focusing or concentrating on a sound, object, visualization, or their breath in effort to increase awareness of the present moment, reduce stress, promote relaxation, and enhance personal and spiritual growth.

I have heard the term *meditate* used loosely throughout my life; however, I did not become intrigued about the true benefits of the process until life became too much for me to bear. Meditation and various forms of it (i.e., mindfulness, yoga, etc.) have become essential to my health and are my way of challenging myself to be intentional about quiet time. In a world that is centered around urgency and immediate gratification, taking time to be present in the moment, enjoying and appreciating the breath you breathe and those in your life has become more of a chore or an item on your to do list instead of the blessing it really is. I tried meditation multiple times, but I would often become frustrated with the frequent fleeting thoughts that would distract me from fully being present in the moment; thus, resulting in me giving up on my attempt. It was not until I had a desperate need for mental peace while navigating the unfamiliar journey of my health challenges that I learned how to properly meditate. Instead of fighting the distracting thoughts, I acknowledged them and imagined myself placing them on a bookshelf with the intention of coming back to them later. Doing this allowed me to: (1) acknowledge that they were real, (2) place value on them and recognize that they too needed my attention, just not at that time, and (3) make mental room to just be present in the moment.

A pivotal point in enhancing this process was applying Lisa Nichols' technique of *Exposing the Lies.* With this technique she instructs you to take 12-16 blank sheets of notebook paper. (You may not use them all.) Using a pencil, begin listing all the things that you have told yourself (with four lines of space between each statement) throughout your life that have created strongholds in your life. She advises that you commit to writing until you dump all the qualifying statements on the paper. However, if you need to take breathers during the process, that is okay. Just try not to exceed a 2-to-3-day timeframe. Once you complete this step, go back to the beginning of the list and for every negative statement, using a red pen, write a positive affirming statement that will help change your view of your circumstances and your future. Once you have written a positive statement for each one, go back and erase all the negative statements you wrote in pencil, leaving only the positive statements in red ink. Read over what are now your new truths, and commit to reading them every day, as many times as necessary. My negative self-talk was so strong that I had to take the process an extra step. I found a scripture in the Bible to support every new truth that I wrote. It was easy for me to doubt myself, but God's word does not return void when coupled with faith. So, my paper looked something like this:

The Lie
~~I'm going to always live check-to-check.~~
~~My mother lived check-to-check. That's all I know.~~

The Truth
My family and I will have multiple streams of income that will enable us to live debt free and be lenders and not borrowers. (Genesis 2:8-15; Deuteronomy 28:12-13)

The Lie
~~Although I have accomplished a lot in my life,~~
~~I have so much to be ashamed of.~~

The Truth
My gift is unique! My story can't be told by anyone else.
I have been groomed to teach in love. (Philippians 4:9)

I even took it another step further and posted my new truths in various places throughout my home, on the dashboard of my car and in my office at work. This is what it took for me to retrain my thoughts about myself, and this in turn helped me embrace the process of meditation in a different way. I still experience distracting thoughts; however, the messages are no longer self-defeating. They're mostly thoughts of things I need to get done, and those things can wait. It took a while for me to improve my technique for meditating, and over time I made changes that better serve me. There is no right or wrong way to meditate. What matters most is that you achieve the opportunity to quiet your mind, releasing yourself from all distractions (even if only for 10 minutes), and allow yourself to be present in that moment that you rest in. That moment that you deserve. I encourage you to try Lisa Nichols' technique. You're welcome to add on my extra steps if necessary. Remember before you can shift your mindset, you must first accept your truth. *"As a man thinketh in his heart, so is he."* *Proverbs 23:7 (NKJV)* As you lean into the shift, you'll find that the opportunities to breathe and rest become more evident.

* * *

Question to Ponder:
What are some ways you can ensure that moments of rest are incorporated into your lifestyle?

_____

_____

_____

_____

_____

_____

_____

_____

_____

_____

_____

_____

_____

_____

_____

_____

_____

*"When you rest, you catch your breath and
it holds you up, like water wings."*
—ANNE LAMOTT

I DARE YOU TO LIVE... AND SHIFT

Before you can shift your mindset, you must first accept your current truths. The truth about how you think. The truth about what or who contributes to those thoughts. The truth about the emotions connected to the events and the people, as well as the impact your truths have had on you throughout your life. This includes how you have treated yourself and others (i.e., friends, acquaintances, and foes) throughout your journey. Negating complete transparency only leads to the creation of emotional baggage. Baggage that, over time, contributes to the evolution of low self-esteem, broken relationships, a lack of self-worth and self-value, financial bondage, and the cycle of generational curses in your life.

The famous Gestalt Psychotherapist, Fritz Perls coined the phrase "peeling the onion" which implies that we must peel back the layers of what we are carrying until our true inner self is revealed. Those layers, also known as baggage, can cause us to become unrecognizable to ourselves, those close to us and even those who are assigned to bless our life. Thus, resulting in hurt and pain lasting longer than we can handle. This process, though often difficult, allows you to shed the things you were never intended to carry, or have carried too long. To fully embrace the process, you must first shift your mind and heart. The shift of these vital parts of your existence must be simultaneous to have a lasting effect. Your heart controls your feelings, and your mind influences your doing. Together they determine your outcomes, your destiny. Increasing your own self-awareness of your true thoughts and feelings about where you are in life helps shape the decisions you make.

Before being diagnosed with Lyme Disease in 2016, I struggled with the symptoms of constant nerve and joint pain, a lack of mental clarity, sleep deprivation, and full body pulsation and lethargy, just to name a few. From the time the symptoms began until about a year and half in, I spent most of the energy I had diagnosing myself on "Dr. Google" and begging God to take the pain away. It was not until I changed how I was allowing myself to process (thoughts) my circumstances, and what I was allowing myself to feel (emotions) about my circumstances that I began to experience a shift in my mental and physical being. There was also a shift in what and to whom I would allow myself to be exposed. A former pastor once said, "Whoever has your ear, has your future."

My research efforts shifted from searching for labels that fit what I was feeling from my *dis*-ease, to searching for the lessons in the process. It is important that you educate yourself while you're in the midst of your shift. Ask questions! Talk to people who have achieved the goal/vision you desire to achieve. Do *reasonable* research. There are a variety of resources out there but be mindful to only gather information from trusted people, websites, or places. Attend workshops and seminars. There are a lot of free or low-cost opportunities out there. Social media has availed endless opportunities to gain information; however, some of those offerings can lead to dead ends, setbacks or exacerbate your situation, so be careful.

Consulting someone is not a sign of weakness; it indicates your desire to make a change and your commitment to gain the necessary knowledge to achieve your wellness goals. As you are gathering information, you must also be careful not become a hoarder of information as this can lead to "analysis paralysis." You will end up having more information than you know what to do with. Organize the information in categories such as these:

- What can I apply now?
    - How is this connected to my goal (to what God has called me to do)?
    - Who are key people that can support me in the application process?
    - What other resources will I need (i.e., time, money, products, etc.)?
    - What's the timeframe for application?

- What can I apply within 3-6 months? 6-9 months? 9-12 months?
    - Ask yourself the same sub-questions listed above to help you add details to your timeframes.

- What do I need to purge to make room?

Purging unnecessary information does not automatically mean you go back to researching new information. It could be that the room created by the purge is to create room for whatever is working well, or an opportunity for you to try what you didn't purge. Allocate a timeframe for gathering and processing, a timeframe for applying, and a set time for assessing your growth. As you move through this process, you will find that you are building a resource toolkit that will consist of those tools that serve you best.

* * *

Question to Ponder:
How is your perspective of any current challenges in
your life benefiting or hindering you?

_____

_____

_____

_____

_____

_____

_____

_____

_____

_____

_____

"When you change the way you look at things,
the things you look at will change."
—WAYNE DYE

I DARE YOU TO LIVE... AND MOVE

The first step towards achieving or maintaining wellness is being willing to do the work, regardless of what the work looks like. Having the goal without the effort (action) to work towards it is pointless. Since the conception of this book, I have started and stopped workout regimens without completing them in the intended timeframes at least ten times. Some of you reading this have probably responded, "Me too!" Others may be thinking, "I just gave up!" The key or secret to success with anything in life is *not* not falling, it's getting back up every time you do. Regardless how many times it happens, GET BACK UP! It is that mentality that led to me going from a size 14 in 2014 to a size 8 in 2018. Yes, it took four years, but I kept trying. The size 8 was a bonus. My goal was a comfortable 10, but my tenacity allowed me to achieve so much more. That is what happens when the tangible is not your soul focus; you often exceed your expectations. Your value shifts from what you are doing to who you are becoming in the process.

Size was not the goal. I just wanted to feel better physically and emotionally. I would have been content with a size 12 if the physical symptoms that consumed me daily stopped. I wanted my joints to stop aching. I no longer wanted to be winded after climbing the stairs in my home. I wanted to be voluntarily active with my growing daughter and enjoy it. I wanted the pain of grief to lessen. I wanted to want to have sex more frequently with my husband again. I wanted to be happy again, just because. I wanted to "want to be" in the presence of family and friends again. I achieved all of it because I kept moving. Not just with exercising, but also in pursuit of real answers. It was my refusal to settle for the prescriptions that were thrown at my symptoms along with *possible* diagnoses that eventually led me to a more accurate diagnosis of Lyme Disease. It was a change in my lifestyle and attitude. My continuous research for cost effective regimens caused me to change what I was eating. I was limiting, and in some cases, excluding foods that promote inflammation and mucus in the body. I focused on increasing my intake of live foods that helped strengthen my immune system, enabling my body to fight harder. I indulged in foods that were mood boosters and became more consistent with exercising (a natural mood booster). I participated in high intensity interval training, yoga, walking and Zumba.

Over the years, I have also consulted and received some guidance and treatment from my general practitioner, a naturopathic doctor, a couple of chiropractors, a medical thermographer, an iridologist, and a womb therapist; all who have played an intricate role during my healing journey. What I have learned along the way are:

1-My body was inflamed long before I was bit by a tick. The Lyme Disease exacerbated what already existed.

2-Medicine is a practice! Nutritional knowledge has not been a part of the foundation of most medical school curricula; hence, why prescriptions are usually the focus of their treatment protocols.

3-I have a God-given right to live as the C.E.O. (Chief Executive Officer) over my health. Decisions about my health are mine, and prevention is my responsibility. I needed and will continue to consult with experts; however, the final decision was and is mine's to make.

4-My grandmother played a vital role in preparing me for such a time like this. I am grateful for the times she allowed me to accompany her on her nature walks, the sabbath lessons she led with me, as well as her firsthand lessons on the benefits of herbs and whole foods.

Exercising and being active are key to optimal living, but today many of us have allowed the pressures of society to prevent us from living a life we truly enjoy. As a child, my brother and I always looked forward to going outside to either play, ride our bikes, shoot hoops, or jump on our trampoline. Once in high school, my choices of physical activity changed from traditional forms of play to being a hyped "Hi-stepper" in D.M. Therrell High School's marching band. In college, it was easier to stay in shape because I walked all over campus. Even after I advanced to off campus living, walking continued to be a best practice for most of us commuters. Once you found a good parking spot on the campus of thee Alabama A&M University, if you were smart, you allowed your car to remain there until your campus affairs were complete for the day. I also had the added benefit of being on my sorority's step team. Those nightly practices helped me burn calories as being a member of one of the local gyms was not as necessary, nor within my very small college budget. Well, at least not until graduate school. Even at that time my decision to become a gym member was in response to a friend's request for my support in their mission to accomplish a lifestyle change. The health benefit was a bonus to the social time. Legends Gym in Tallahassee, FL often mirrored the scene of a Day Party. I maintained the membership until I completed my graduate studies and relocated.

Fast forward to reality! It was not until after I started my first job in my career that I had to really "move to live." When I noticed the first sign of cellulite, I told myself that the gym fee not being in the budget could no longer be an excuse to not exercise. I began to go for walks with short—*very short*— spurts of running. I also took advantage of trial memberships offered by local fitness centers. When the free period ended, I resorted back to hitting the pavement with Tom & Jerry, my feet. That lasted a couple of years, and served the purpose of physical and mental wellness, at least B.C. (Before Child) I continued with my workout regimen until my second trimester of pregnancy.

Once my daughter was born, I did not have the time, energy, or motivation to develop nor engage in a workout regimen. My schedule was inundated with being a mother, a wife, and a professional school counselor; all while trying to maintain my sanity amongst the three roles. What I did not realize at the time was even twenty minutes of exercise/fitness a day for three times a week would have helped me manage my life better than I was doing. The overwhelming newness to motherhood, the necessity to financially contribute to my household and the "for better or worse" of being a wife had begun to take a toll on me. I was headed right into a pit that I was unaware existed until I landed in it.

Benefits of Exercise/Structured Fitness:

Well, we all know at least 2 or 3 physical benefits, such as: building muscle, improving heart health, and decreasing body fat. But what we often overlook or are unaware of are the other much-needed mental health benefits of moving regularly.

1. Stress Reduction: Exercising increases concentrations of norepinephrine, a chemical that can moderate the brain's response to stress.

2. Boost Happy Chemicals: Exercising releases endorphins, which create feelings of happiness and euphoria. I asked myself, antidepressant pill or exercise? *Hmmmm...*

3. Improve Self Confidence: Regardless of weight, size, gender or age, exercise can quickly elevate a person's negative perception of self-worth.

4. Enjoying the Great Outdoors: Exercising outdoors can increase self-esteem, boost confidence and happiness. It also increases your exposure to fresh air. Indoor air can be more toxic than the great outdoors.

5. Prevent Cognitive Decline: Although exercise has not been proven to cure degenerative diseases that affect the brain, it can help strengthen your body's defense mechanisms against cognitive decline by boosting the necessary chemicals in the brain that support and prevent degeneration of the hippocampus, an important part of the brain for memory and learning.

6. Sharpen Your Memory: Physical activity that increases your heart rate and causes you to break a sweat increases your memory and your ability to

learn new skills. It does not have to be a fitness class. Think outside the box, and enjoy a dance class, game of freeze tag, dodgeball, or hopscotch with the kids. Don't have kids? Grab a friend's, neighbor's or relative's child.

7. Help Alleviate Anxiety: Just a 20-minute jog or workout intervals releases warm and fuzzy chemicals that can help people with anxiety disorders calm down and reduce anxiety sensitivity.

8. Boost Brain Power: Do you want more brain power? Well, increase your cardiovascular exercise! Research indicates that cardiovascular exercise can create new brain cells (a.k.a neurogenesis) and improve overall brain performance.

(Resources: https://greatist.com/fitness/13-awesome-mental-health-benefits-exercise & https://www.huffingtonpost.com/2013/03/27/mental-health-benefits-exercise_n_2956099.html)

Our movement matters! Not just for our physical wellness, but in every aspect of our lives. Becoming stagnant or paralyzed in our work towards that which we desire to have, is merely a wish, a desire to do or have something with no movement. When we add action to the wish, we no longer remain in the position we started in. Adding action propels you closer to your goal. You can change your relationships, your career path or business ideas by first changing who you are, or how you show up in those areas of your life. When you move in a direction that attracts wholeness and healing, growth and strength are inevitable. Change who you are, and your life will follow. Before you add one more thing to your to-do list, ask yourself these questions to determine if you will be committed to conducting the required actions that will help you *move* in the right direction.

- How important is this to me?
- Is it within my power to make this happen through my own actions? If not, who can I consult with for support? What's my next step?
- Is this something that I have the potential to do, or is it a part of my God-given purpose?

It's the movement that makes it a reality. Your commitment to putting action behind your goals is not only an investment in your life, but also an investment in the lives of those you love...adding quality to your years, and the time we spend together. **Get up and move!**

* * *

Questions to Ponder:
What are you willing to sacrifice to achieve a healthier you?
What goal or vision might you not see come to
fruition if you don't get up and move?

_____

_____

_____

_____

_____

_____

_____

_____

_____

_____

_____

_____

"Your health is your is wealth; live like it."
—CHOSEN

AT LAST...

God. No Clock. No Calendar. No Box.

In life, we are taught and reminded that if we want to be successful, we must plan for success. This planning often includes timeframes, a plan B and C in the event plan A falls through, as well as a list of necessary resources. We are also taught to plan for the worst that could happen with the intention that the plan will help us navigate through the challenges that accompany this journey called life. I reference 1 Peter 5:6 (NKJV) again because it is so powerful in the way it instructs us to humble ourselves under God's mighty hand, that He may exalt us in due time. To humble ourselves means to stop and take a break from trying to have the answer/solution to our challenges and seek God's guidance. When we seek His guidance we must also trust His timing hence the "due time." Trusting God's timing requires us to cast our cares (i.e., the things that we are worried about, the things we try to plan for, etc.) upon Him because He cares for us. God's care and concern for us is everlasting!

As the planner of my family, it's not unusual for me to pull out one of my calendars which includes the one in my phone, the work schedule, and the house commitments. I learned earlier in life that for me to stay on top of things and prevent as much chaos as possible, I had to utilize some form of graphic organizer. Utilizing calendars helped me throughout my secondary and post-secondary educational journeys. They have helped me throughout the progression of my career and in managing my life as a wife and a mother. Additionally, they have worked well to keep my social life organized. Although planning and organizing have been a key factor to my successes, it has not been as beneficial in helping me prepare for or manage my greatest challenges, or shall I say the lowest blows of my life.

I was raised by a God-fearing mother and praying grandmother who both frequently quoted God's word during our conversations. However, it wasn't until I had to endure great losses and a health challenge that I realized that it was going to take more than memorizing scripture. I now needed to connect to the Word and God himself in a way that I hadn't done before. It was then that I began to learn how to replace my begging and pleading in my prayers with speaking God's word back to Him. Strength was not gained immediately, but it was definitely evident over time. As each emotional tunnel was brightened through His spiritual light, the weight of my world became lighter, and oxygen began to flow in the bubble that once slowly suffocated the joy of life out of me. I perceived this second wind was God's way of daring me to live on purpose. Since I had already experienced some great lows, staying there, or getting back up were my only two options. I chose to get back up, but this time, instead of trying to hide or dress up my pain, I allowed others to witness my healing process. I purposely did this so they too would know that it was only by God's grace that I was able to rise out of my pit. That same God is ready and available for you to access for your journey. Just ask! **Isaiah 55:9** (*NKJV*) reminds us that his thoughts are not our thoughts; nor his ways our ways. Therefore, we cannot confine him to our timelines and expectations.

It is my hope that you were able to connect with me at some point throughout this reading. I don't take lightly the time you've invested in reading about my journey and pray that your journey is consumed with the peace of God which surpasses all understanding

MEET THE COACH

Tuere Dunton-Forbes, a Georgia native, currently resides in Charlotte, North Carolina with her supportive husband Marcelles and their spirited daughter, Amari. She earned a B.A. in Psychology from Alabama A&M University and a M.Ed. in School Counseling from Florida A&M University. Passionate about helping others, she has worked in one of the local school systems as a professional school counselor since 2005. Her interest in making health and wellness a priority to her lifestyle was birthed out of the death of both of her parents (2013 & 2016) to preventable diseases and an attack on her own health for which was later diagnosed as Lyme disease. Enduring those losses while withstanding her own health challenges has given her the desire to be a better steward of her temple so that she can be an example and educate others on how to do the same. Though it's unfortunate that many wait until they are given a diagnosis before making the decision to make prevention a priority in life, Tuere believes that small steps can make a BIG difference, as she is living proof. As a result, she obtained her Health Coaching certification via the completion of the Dr. Sears Wellness Institute's science-based program (2016) and founded her life and wellness coaching brand (N360). She uses her knowledge and personal experiences to empower others to strategies that can help them live as the C.E.O. of their lives, while showing them how to connect life and wellness, one commitment at a time. Learn more about Tuere at www.n360life.com.

CPSIA information can be obtained
at www.ICGtesting.com
Printed in the USA
BVHW010033280522
638356BV00002B/10

9 781737 641162